D0046237

SCOTLAND

Colin Baxter Photography, Grantown-on-Spey, Scotland

GAADA STACK, FOULA, SHETLAND

The stacks and sheer cliffs of the most isolated inhabited island in the British Isles are continuously eroded by the power of the waves. A Site of Special Scientific Interest, the Norse called it *Fugl-oy*, 'the island of birds', and Foula's populations of puffins, guillemots, razorbills and shags are almost too numerous to count.

THE OLD MAN OF ▶ HOY, ORKNEY

A challenge to generations of rock climbers, the Old Man of Hoy, a free-standing red sandstone stack, towers above the nearby cliffs to 450 ft (137 m). St John's Head to the north, at over 1000 ft (305 m), was not successfully climbed until 1970. Hoy is the second largest and most mountainous of the 70 or so Orkney islands; *Haey* in Norse means 'High island'. Many native trees flourish in its sheltered gullies. To the north-east of Hoy is the once-important naval anchorage of Scapa Flow.

◀ CASTLE STALKER, APPIN, ARGYLL

Like so many of Scotland's castles, Stalker is a square-set, sturdy tower house built to withstand attack by both ferocious weather and fearsome assailants. It has three storeys over a pit prison. The castle was probably built for James VI about 1540 by his kinsman, Duncan Stewart of Appin, as a hunting lodge and to confirm his presence in the area. The castle was lost by the Stewarts several times; once even forfeited to a Campbell when Duncan Stewart gambled the castle for an eight-oared galley.

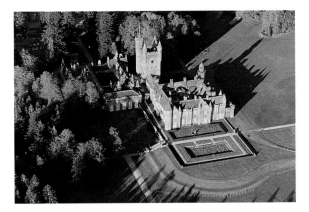

BALMORAL CASTLE, DEESIDE

Queen Victoria and Prince Albert's mutual love for the Highlands led them to search for a place to stay on their regular autumn holidays. They found the Balmoral estate, where Prince Albert created a new castle to supercede the existing house. Completed in 1856, its baronial turrets of white granite still glow amidst the surrounding woodland.

◀ PARK CIRCUS & PARK QUADRANT, KELVINGROVE, GLASGOW

Park conservation area, with its long honey-coloured terraces, is a fine example of Victorian architecture and planning. The curved forms of Park Circus, Place, Terrace and Quadrant were designed in the 1850s, with French architectural details, by Charles Wilson. Four towers pierce the skyline, the most distinctive, a campanile.

LUSKENTYRE, HARRIS ▶

The spectacular stretches of white sand on Harris's Atlantic coast contrast with the peaty lochans and barren rocky landscape of most of the island. Today, the words 'Harris Tweed' ensure that this island is known across the world.

CARRBRIDGE, STRATHSPEY

This memorable single-span, rubble-built Bridge of Carr was originally constructed by the Seafield Estate in 1717 across the Dulnain River, and gives its name to the village. Carrbridge lies within reach of the Cairngorms, Britain's highest range of mountains and one of its last truly wild areas.

The Cairngorm Mountains, Strathspey

Ben Nevis, Lochaber

Britain's highest mountain at 4406 ft (1343 m). On one face, a rounded, contoured mountain, on the other an incised rock face of stark, remarkable beauty. Many visitors wish only to walk to its summit, others endeavour to conquer one of the most formidable and extensive rock climbs in Britain.

Iona Abbey ▶ Church

The enduring fame of the small island of Iona was ensured when St Columba founded his monastery here in 563. Having left Ireland with 12 companions, Iona became a base for his missionary work to convert the people, of what is now Scotland, to Christianity. Today, Iona is a sacred pilgrimage site visited by many thousands of people annually. The religious foundation survived despite the predations of the Norse and later destruction during the Reformation.

◀ THE BORDERS

Scotland's borderlands were the scene of centuries of warfare, raiding and devastation. The landscape here is gentler and more rounded than the Highlands to the north, but the history is perhaps even more consistently bloody. From the end of the 13th century, for 400 years, cross-border violence came in the form of raids and full-scale invasions. Some of these were immortalised in the famous Border Ballads, one of the best-known of which commemorates the Battle of Otterburn in 1388.

PORTNAHAVEN, ISLAY

Originally a community of lobster fishermen and farm workers, Portnahaven was founded in 1788 and lies at the southern end of the Rhinns peninsula of Islay, the most southerly and fertile island of the Inner Hebrides. Islay is different. Unlike its mountainous neighour, Jura, it is a softer, greener island, relatively mild due to the effects of the Gulf Stream.

URQUHART CASTLE & LOCH NESS

Most of the remaining ruins of this once-great castle, including the lofty tower house, date from after 1509. The castle stands on the west shore of Loch Ness and guards the north-eastern end of the once strategically important Great Glen.

THE CUILLIN HILLS & LOCH DHÙGHAILL, SKYE

Looking north-west across Loch Dhùghaill on the Sleat peninsula, the
jagged ridge of the Cuillin Hills form one of the most exciting skylines in Britain.

◀ CALANAIS STANDING STONES, LEWIS

This mysterious stone circle was built some 4000 years ago.

PITTENWEEM, FIFE

'The place of the cave', reputedly St Fillan's, Pittenweem is the principal fishing village in the East Neuk of Fife and home of most of the East Fife fishing fleet. One of a series of medieval harbours described by James VI as, 'the fringe of gold on a grey cloth mantle'. Red pantiles and crow-stepped gables characterise these once-bustling fishing villages.

ST ANDREWS, ▶ FIFE

Once the ecclesiastical capital of Scotland, and certainly the golfing capital of the world, St Andrews is imbued with superlatives: the earliest university, founded in 1412; the oldest and largest cathedral, begun in 1161, and consecrated in the presence of Robert the Bruce in 1318; its interior was destroyed in 1559 during the Protestant Reformation.

The Royal and Ancient Golf Club was first formed in 1754, and founded where golf had been played since the 12th century.

◄ RUM FROM NEAR ARISAIG

Famous for its sea eagles, alpine plants and red deer. In the 15th century Rum, the largest of the Small Isles of the Inner Hebrides, was exchanged by the Clanranalds for the great galley of MacLean of Coll; apparently they tried to renege when they found the timbers of the boat were rotten! A spectacular, mountainous island, its population was decimated in the 19th century when sheep were introduced and the people 'cleared' and shipped to Nova Scotia.

EILEAN DONAN CASTLE

Eilean Donan, 'island of Donan', a 7th-century Celtic monk. A castle was built here about 1220, where Loch Alsh meets Loch Duich, for defence against Vikings. During the 1719 Jacobite Rising, the castle was ruined in a bombardment by Government frigates. Between 1912 and 1932, nearly a quarter of a million pounds was spent on its restoration.

SCOTLAND

Scotland is a land of many contrasts. Most famously, perhaps, is the difference between the Highlands and the Lowlands, so clearly divided by the Highland Boundary Fault which runs south-west from Stonehaven to Helensburgh.

Scotland embodies a huge variety of landscapes in a relatively small space. The features are perhaps not as large as their equivalents on the great continental land-masses, but the mountains are no less dramatic, the beaches no less curvaceous. From Lowland to Highland, Scotland's landscapes can evolve from green rolling pasture to stark mountain wilderness, often across short distances.

East and west also show marked contrasts; where the rugged beauty of the western coastline is washed by the mild waters of the Atlantic Gulf Stream, the more fertile eastern shores are frequently exposed to biting winds and cold fogs or 'haars' which roll in to envelop the landscape.

Whether your preference is for the quilted pattern of fields on the Howe of the Mearns, or the fragile Gaada Stack off Shetland, or for the elegant crescents of Georgian and Victorian city centres, this book features many of the faces of Scotland that make the country unique. Some, like the Forth Rail Bridge or Ben Nevis, need no introduction; others, less well known, like the fishing village of Portnahaven, are here for you to discover.

STACKS OF DUNCANSBY, CAITHNESS

The rock stacks and geos, wave-torn from the cliffs of Duncansby Head, make a dramatic coastline at the north-eastern tip of Scotland. Edged with rough, wind-stunted grasses, the 200 ft (60 m) cliffs are home to a myriad of seabirds. For the lighthouse, and nearby John o' Groats, there is little shelter from the winds off the Pentland Firth.

STONEHAVEN ▶ & EAST COAST FROM THE AIR

The once-thriving fishing village clings to the shore which adjoins the rich farmlands of the Howe of the Mearns, made famous by Lewis Grassic Gibbon's *Sunset Song*. On the pier stands the 16th-century Tolbooth, built originally to store supplies for nearby Dunnottar Castle. In 1652 the crown jewels of Scotland were safely smuggled from Dunnottar by two local women out of the grasp of Cromwell's army, and buried in nearby Kinneff Church.

◀ LOCH CRERAN, ARGYLL

One of the many long-fingered sea lochs stretching into the west coast of Argyll, it lies on the north side of Benderloch, *Beinn-eadhar-da-loch*, a mountain chain between two arms of the sea. The other arm is Loch Etive.

North of Loch Creran is Appin where, in 1752, Colin Campbell of Glenure was slain in the notorious 'Appin murder', which was later made famous by Robert Louis Stevenson. At the head of the loch is Beinn Sgulaird, 3059 ft (932 m), one of the Lorn Munros.

OBAN HARBOUR, ARGYLL

Gateway to the Hebrides. Oban prospered late in the 19th century: with the advent of the railway and steam-ships, visitors flocked to the town to sail to the Hebrides, and east or south by way of the Caledonian and Crinan canals. The unlikely skyline silhouette of the Colosseum is a replica known as McCaig's Tower or Folly.

BEN CRUACHAN, ▶
ARGYLL

In the heart of Campbell country, 'Cruachan' was the war cry of Clan Campbell. Only 400 million years old, the Caledonian granite which rises into the seven peaks of Cruachan, 'the haunch of peaks', high above the Cruachan Reservoir and the Pass of Brander, is relatively young. One peak rises above the others to form the Ben at 3672 ft (1119 m). This great mountain dominates the 24-mile- (39-km-) long Loch Awe, one of Scotland's largest freshwater lochs, which also boasts some of the tallest tales for the size of its legendary brown trout.

Inside the mountain, thousands of feet below the Ben, is the power house for the Loch Awe hydroelectric scheme, opened in 1965.

◄ THE FORTH BRIDGE

Now one of the world's great landmarks, the Forth Rail Bridge stands at the Queensferry Narrows spanning the waters of the Firth of Forth. Ceremoniously completed by the Prince of Wales (later Edward VII), when he drove-in the last of 8 million rivets on 4 March 1890, it was the pinnacle of 19th-century British engineering.

The longest cantilever bridge in Britain, at over 1½ miles (2.4 km) across with headroom of 156 ft (47.5 m) for the shipping beneath, its construction took about 4500 men over 7 years; 57 were killed.

In 1992 it became the biggest illuminated bridge in the world with over 1000 floodlights on 25 miles (40 km) of cable.

Loch Torridon from Beinn Alligin, Wester Ross

Published in Great Britain in 1999 by Colin Baxter Photography Ltd,
Grantown-on-Spey, Moray PH26 3NA, Scotland

Reprinted 2000, 2002, 2004   Text by Lorna Ewan

Photographs & Text Copyright © Colin Baxter 1999, 2004   All rights reserved.

A CIP Catalogue record for this book is available from the British Library.

ISBN 1-84107-006-8   *Colin Baxter Gift Book Series*   Printed in Hong Kong

Page one photograph: **Blair Castle**   Page two photograph: **Buachaille Etive Mór, Glencoe**
Front cover photograph: **Loch Lomond from the air**   Back cover photograph: **Loch Laggan, Badenoch**

▲ Loch Shiel, Lochaber   Loch Assynt, Sutherland ▶

EDINBURGH CASTLE & CITY AT DUSK

Scotland's capital. Its unmistakable skyline is dominated by the castle perched
high on the dark crag of Castle Rock. This fortified site, probably inhabited for at least
the last 7000 years, formed the nucleus from which the city of Edinburgh developed.